THE APPLE
and Other Fruits

By the Same Author and Photographer

The Carrot and Other Root Vegetables
Maple Tree
Milkweed
Peanut
The Tomato and Other Fruit Vegetables
Vegetables from Stems and Leaves

THE APPLE and Other Fruits

BY MILLICENT E. SELSAM

photographs by Jerome Wexler

William Morrow and Company

New York 1973

Text copyright © 1973 by Millicent E. Selsam
Photographs copyright © 1973 by Jerome Wexler
(except as noted in acknowledgments for photographs)

All rights reserved. No part of this book may be reproduced or utilized in any form or by any means, electronic or mechanical, including photocopying, recording or by any information storage and retrieval system, without permission in writing from the Publisher. Inquiries should be addressed to William Morrow and Company, Inc.,
105 Madison Ave., New York, N.Y. 10016.
Printed in the United States of America.

Library of Congress Catalog Card Number 73-4928
ISBN 0-688-20089-3
ISBN 0-688-30089-8 (lib. bdg.)

3 4 5

Acknowledgments for Photographs

Arthur Ambler, National Audubon Society, 44
Jack Dermid, National Audubon Society, 42
Maurice and Sally Landre, National Audubon Society, 45
Richard Parker, National Audubon Society, 43
Sunkist Growers, Inc., 46
United States Department of Agriculture, 47

The author and photographer thank Dr. Howard S. Irwin,
Executive Director of the New York Botanical Gardens,
for checking the text and photographs of this book.
They also thank Barnes Orchards, Inc., Wallingford, Connecticut,
for its assistance to the photographer.

Apples grow on apple trees.
Here is an apple tree in the winter.
From what part of the tree
do the apples grow?

In the spring the apple blossoms appear. We have to look at these flowers to find out where the fruit comes from. The flowers are pink when they first open and then change to white.

The petals are pretty, but the important parts of the flower are in the center. Without them no apples would develop.

When the petals are removed, you can see these important parts. One kind are called "stamens." The stamens are clustered in a ring around five taller parts. Each stamen has a pollen bag, called an "anther," at the top. The five taller parts in the center are the top of what is called the "pistil." They end in sticky "stigmas," which later receive the pollen.

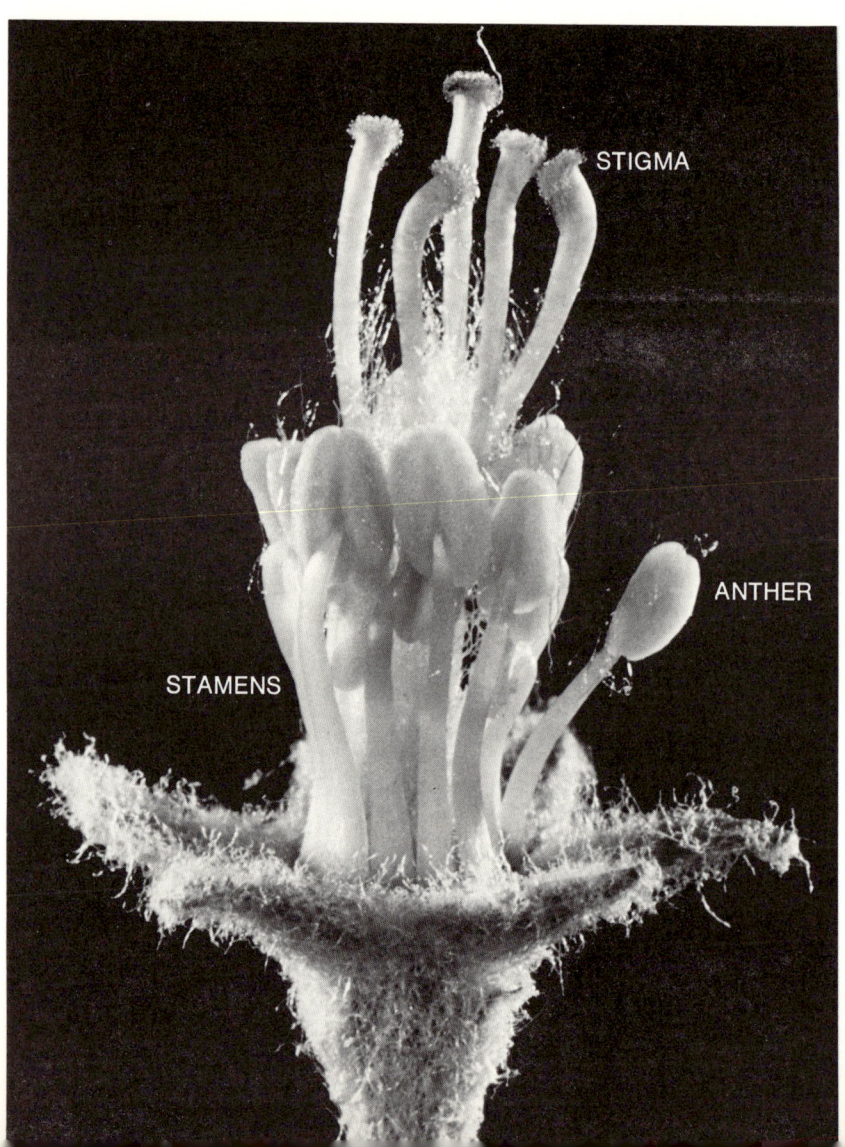

As the flower ripens, the stamens grow taller and the stigmas spread out. Here you can see the bottom of the pistil, which is called the "ovary." The parts between the stigmas and the ovary are called "styles."

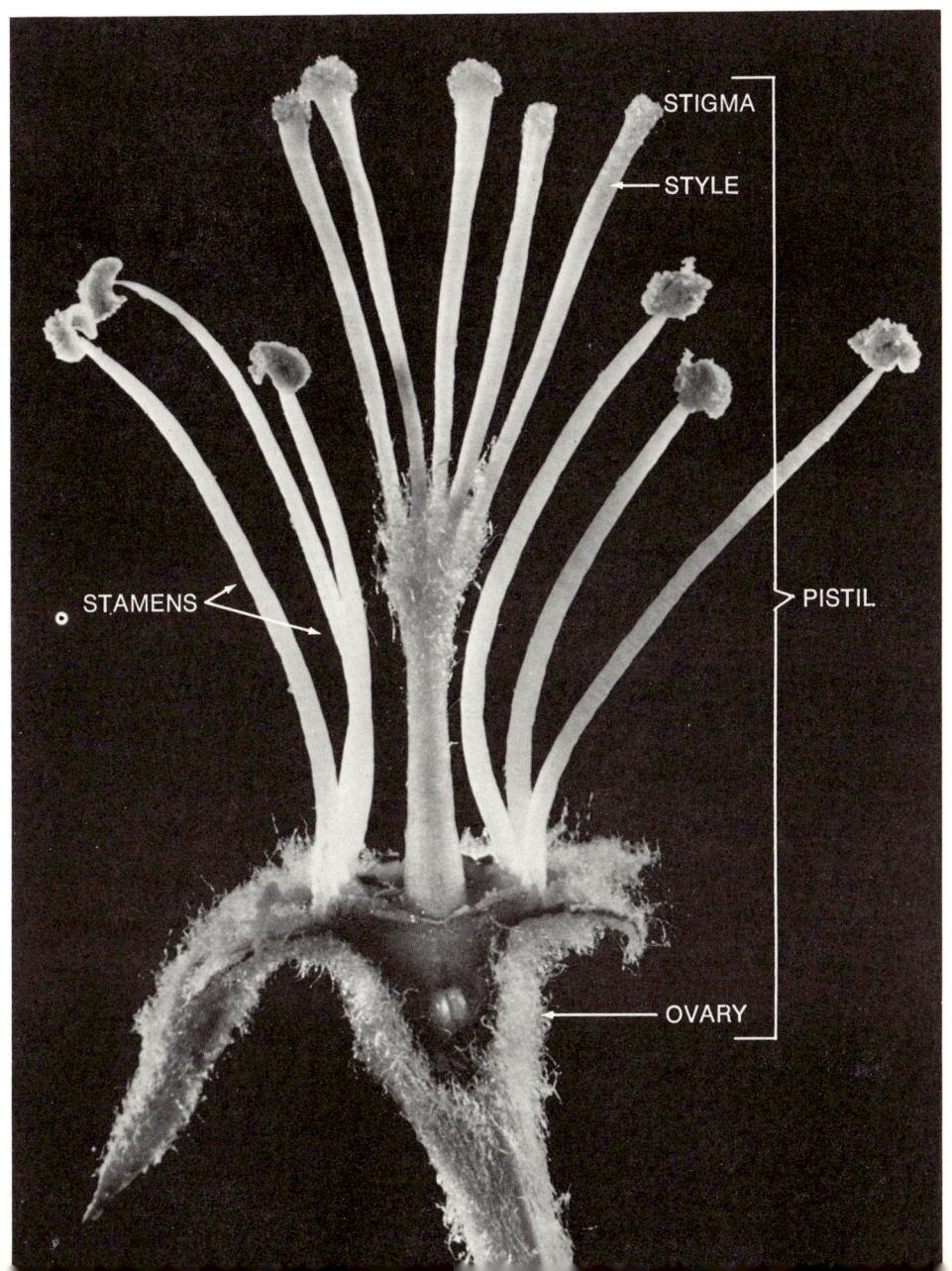

The ovary is imbedded in a cuplike part. Inside the ovary there are seeds-to-be, called "ovules." They become seeds if they are fertilized, or joined, by the contents of a pollen grain.

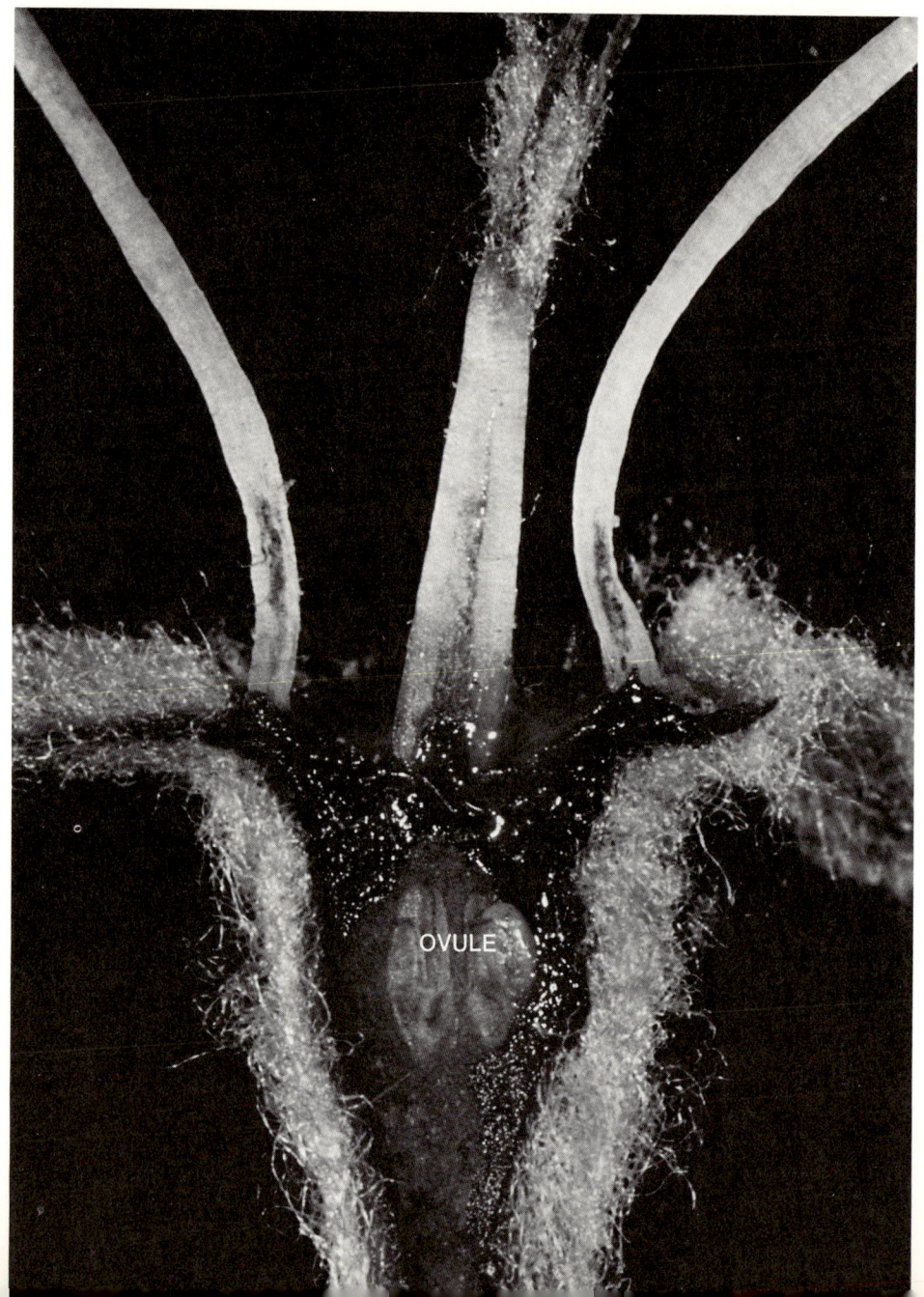

13

Each anther contains about 3500 pollen grains. There are 20 stamens in each flower, so one apple flower contains about 70,000 pollen grains.

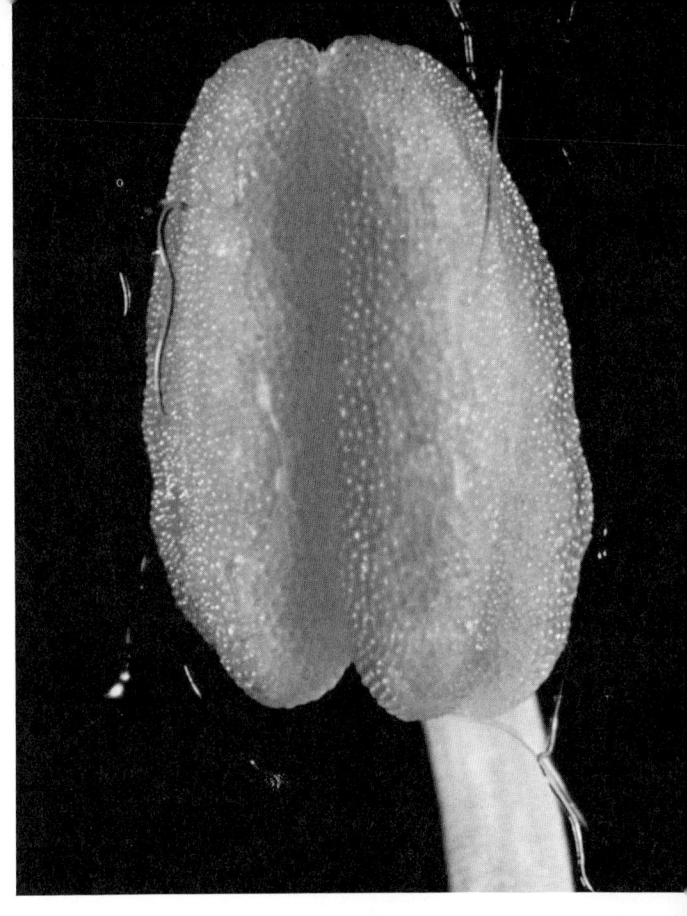

When the petals are wide open, the pollen comes out of the anthers.

Apple flowers are sweet, and they produce a flower juice called "nectar." Insects, mostly bees, come to suck the nectar and gather pollen. When they land on the flowers, their hairs get dusted with sticky pollen. Then they fly to the next flower, where they accidentally brush the pollen grains onto the sticky stigmas. When pollen is transferred in this way, from the stamen to the pistil, a process called "pollination" takes place.

Honeybees fly only if the temperature is above sixty-five degrees and if it is not raining or especially windy. The time is short when the weather is just right for flying and the apple blossoms are open. For this reason, apple growers put beehives in orchards to make sure there will be enough bees around when pollination is possible.

When pollen grains reach the stigmas, they send out tubes. The tubes grow down from the stigmas through the styles to the ovary where the ovules are. The contents of each pollen tube join with an ovule. When this happens, the ovules are fertilized and can develop into seeds.

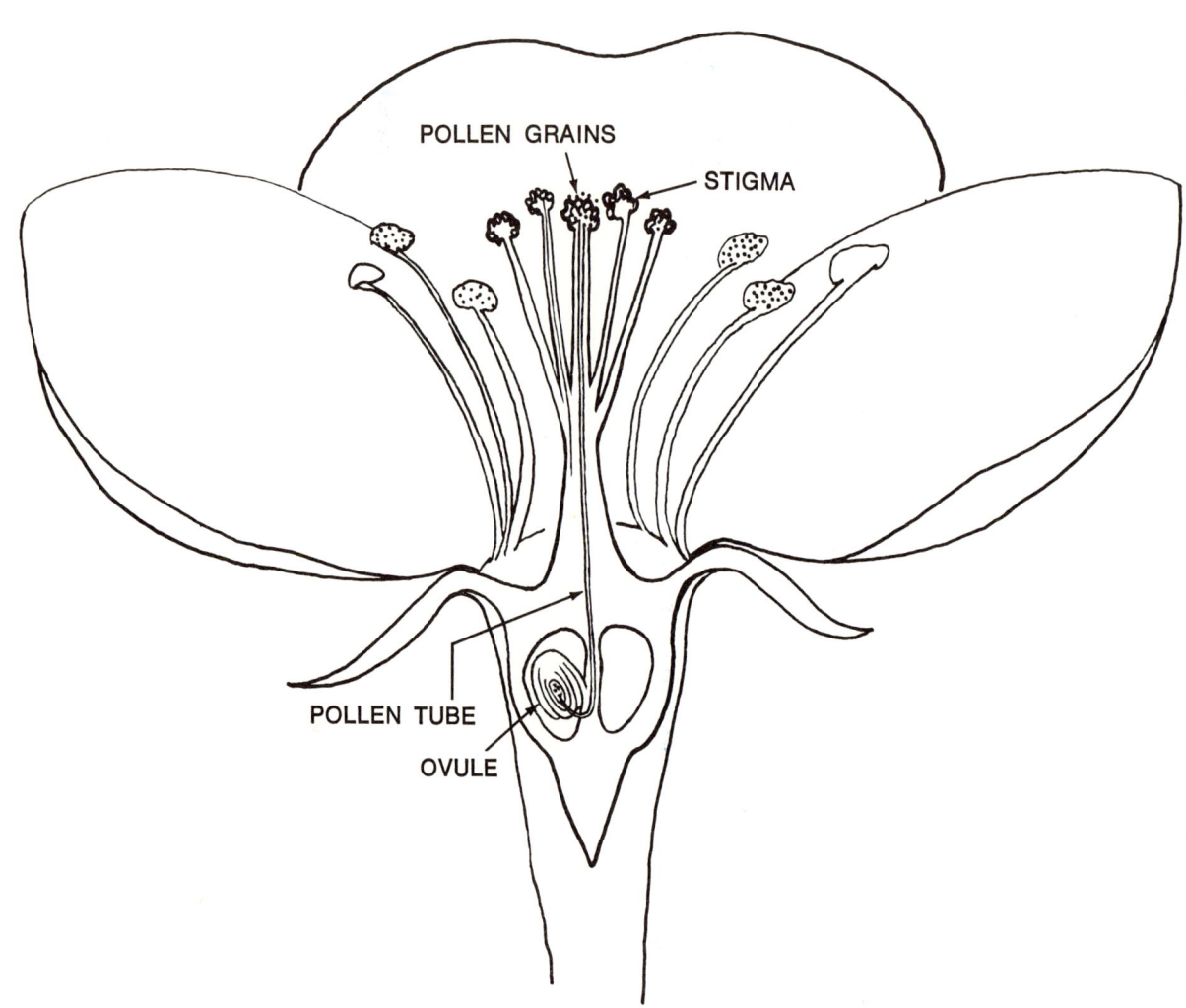

The flower fades, the stamens wither, and the petals fall. But even though an apple tree at this time looks like a mass of leaves, the ovaries and the cuplike parts around them are left behind where the flowers were.

The ovaries and the cuplike parts have begun to swell into apples. The stamens, the styles, and the stigmas are drying up. Inside the ovary you can see the ovules starting to change into seeds. If no pollination has taken place, the flowers will drop or develop into a small fruit that drops early.

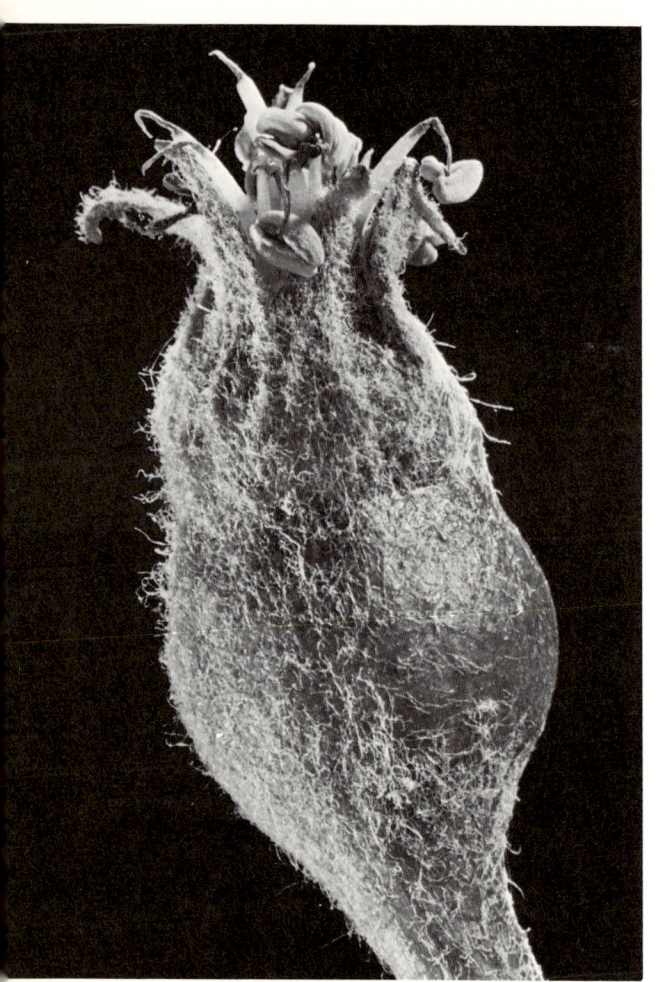

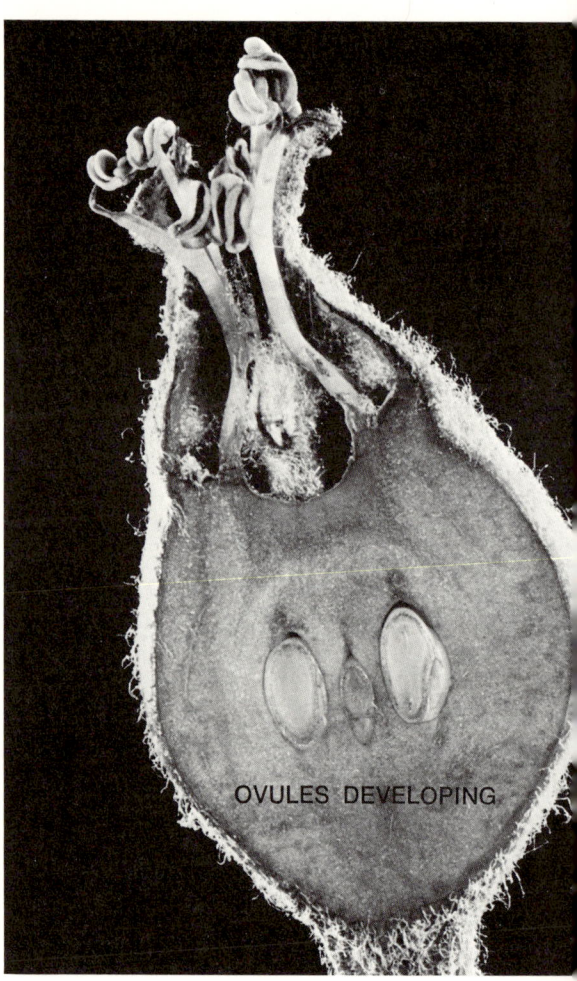

OVULES DEVELOPING

But the fertilized apple ovaries and surrounding parts grow bigger and bigger.

They become ripe red apples.

If you cut an apple in half, you can see near the core five chambers that contain the seeds.

If all the ovules are fertilized, there will be about ten seeds. But often you will find fewer seeds because some ovules are not fertilized. This apple is lopsided because the ovules on one side were not fertilized and the tissues around them did not swell as much as they did on the other side, where the ovules were fertilized. Apples can be lopsided for other reasons too.

Usually apples are thinned, which means that some are removed so that the others can grow bigger. Growers thin their apples so that they are eight inches apart. In these pictures the leaves have been removed so that you can see the apples.

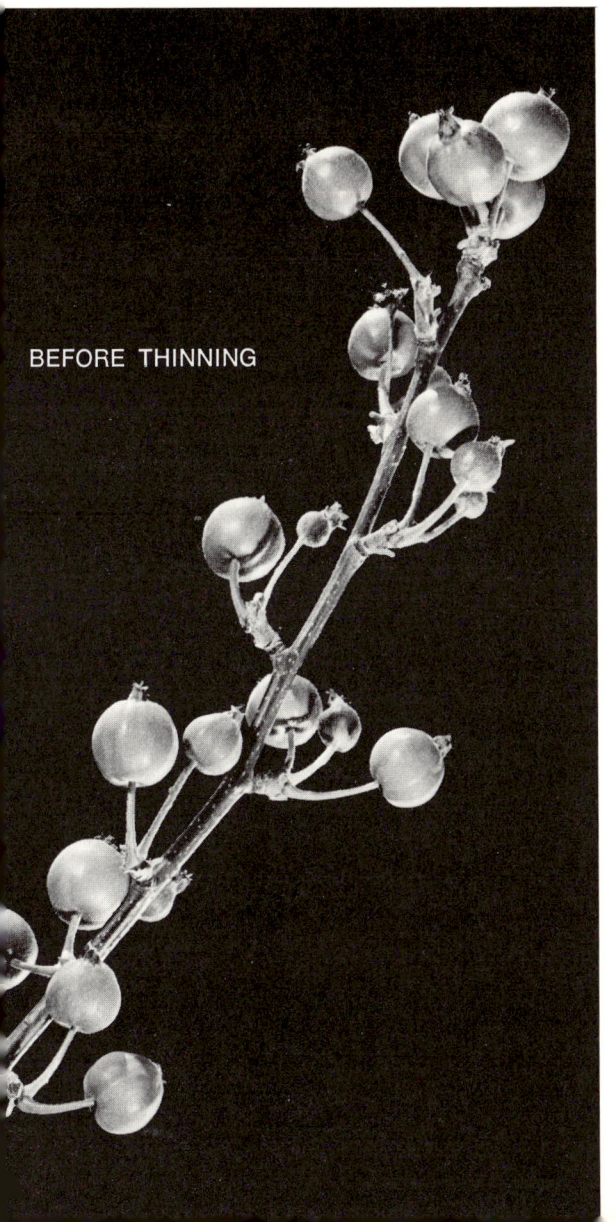

BEFORE THINNING

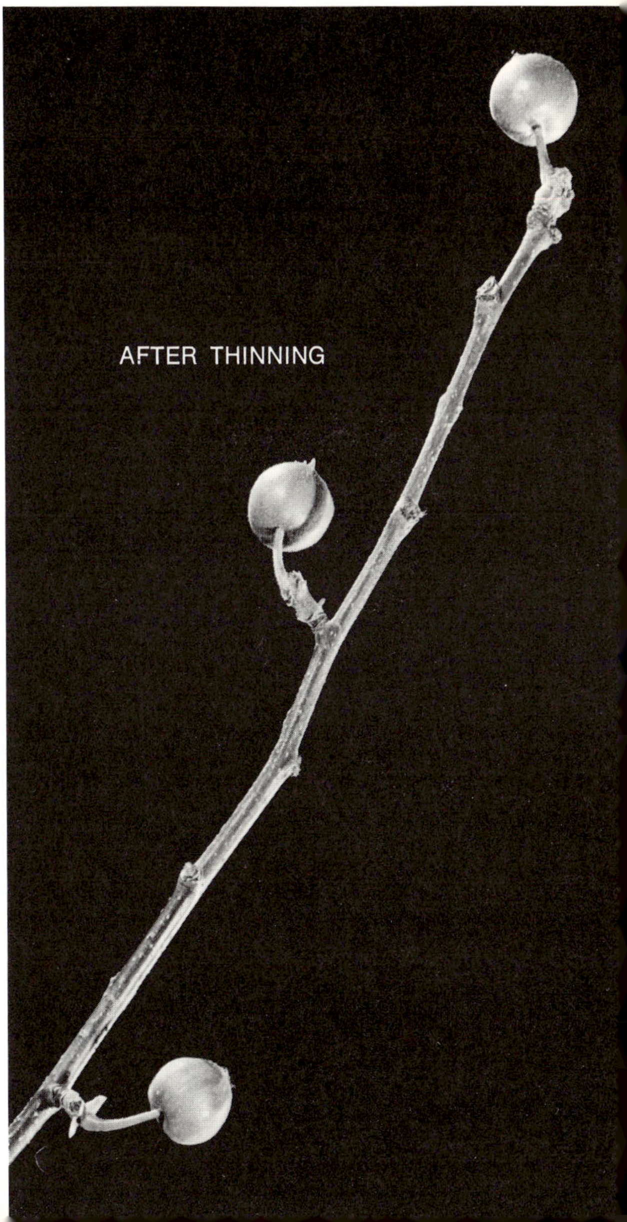

AFTER THINNING

You can plant apple seeds, and they will grow into apple trees. But first the seeds have to ripen in a moist, cold place. You can put apple seeds on moist paper in a jar, cover them with more moist paper, and put the jar in the refrigerator. If you keep the paper moist, the seeds will sprout in six to eight weeks. During this ripening, chemical changes take place in the seeds that enable them to sprout.

But the seeds of an apple tree cannot be depended on to reproduce the very same sort of apple as grew on the parent tree. If 100 trees are grown from the seeds of one tree, many of them will bear small, sour fruit.

When Johnny Appleseed planted apple seeds in Ohio and Indiana, most of the trees that grew from his seeds did not bear good fruit. But some were good, and this fruit was spread in two ways: by "grafting" and by "budding."

When a grower grafts, he cuts off the top of a growing tree whose roots are strong and resistant to frost and disease. Then he places in the cut a woody shoot bearing one or more buds.

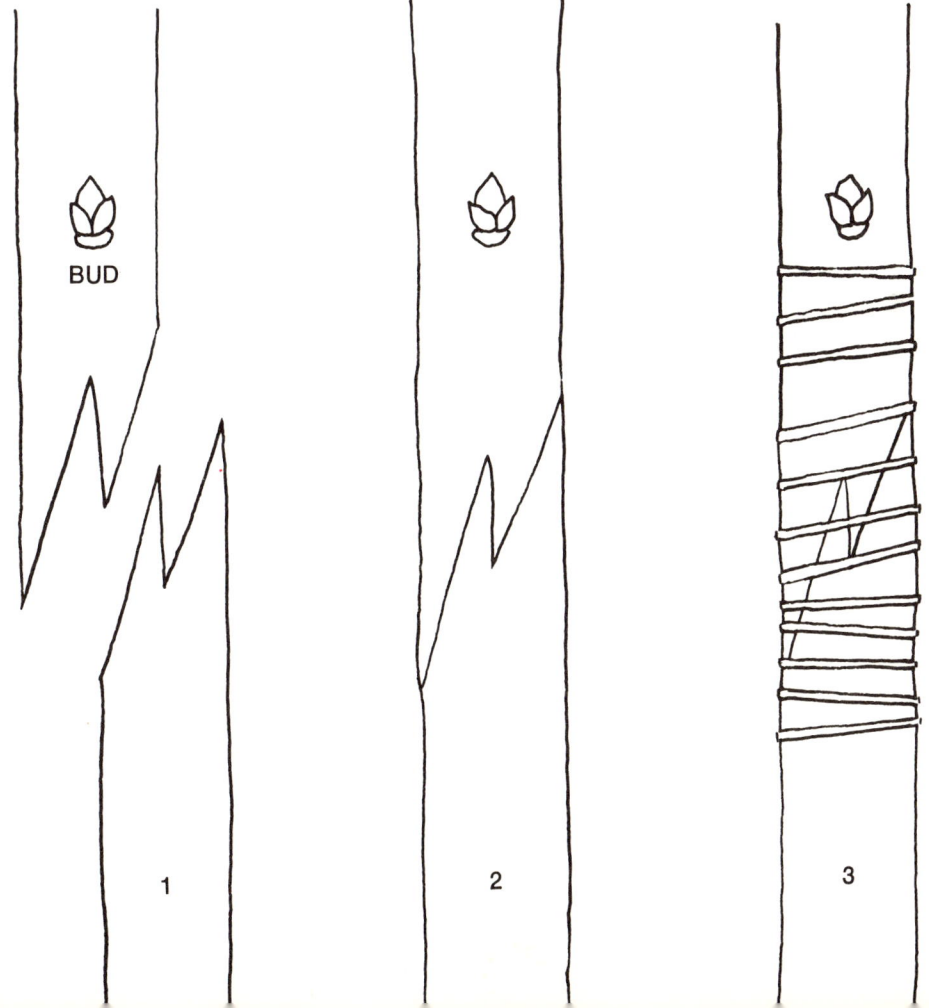

When a grower buds, he places only one bud beneath the cut bark of a young tree.

In time the two cut parts grow together.

Only the branches growing from the graft or bud are allowed to grow. The rest are cut back.
From the twig or bud a whole new treetop grows. And it produces exactly the same kind of fruit as it would have done if it had not been removed from the parent tree.

In this picture you can see exactly where a Golden Delicious branch was grafted onto the stub of a young tree. The tree now will bear only Golden Delicious apples.

Apples have to be picked off the tree. Then they are put into boxes and kept in cold storage until they are sent to market.

Pears develop from flowers just as apples do. The flowers look like apple blossoms.

In the picture above, the petals have been pulled off so that you can see the stamens and the stigmas. The ovary is below them and is imbedded in a cuplike part just as the apple is.

Pear flowers also are pollinated by bees.

After pollination, fertilization of the ovules takes place and the fleshy parts around the ovules begin to change into a fruit. The fruits get bigger and bigger until they are full-grown pears.

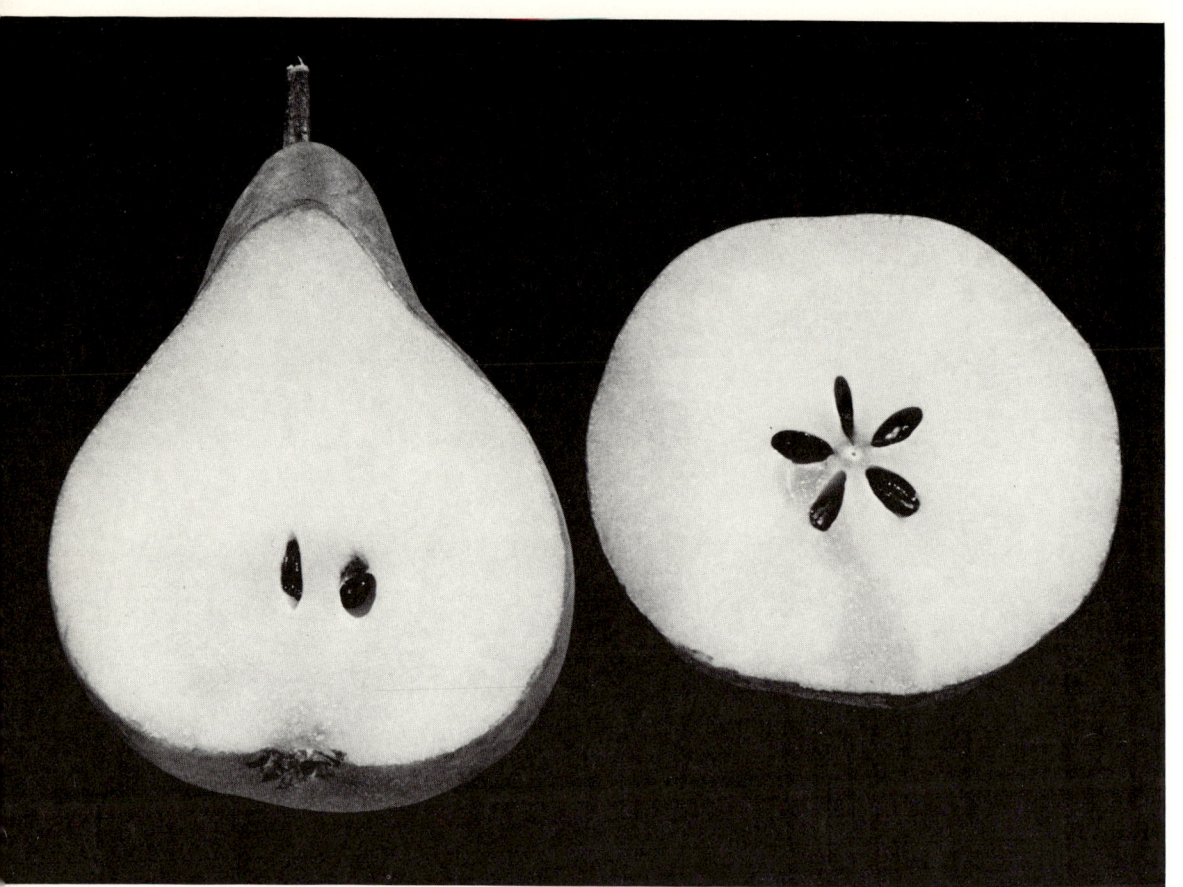

If you cut through a pear, you can see the seeds. Like apple seeds, these seeds sprout if they are kept moist and cold.

But the seed of pear trees also cannot be depended on to produce the same sort of pear as grew on the parent tree. So pear branches or buds are grafted onto young trees with good roots.

YOUNG PEAR TREE GROWING FROM SEED

Peach flowers appear on a peach tree before the leaves. They may be white or shades of pink or red. Notice the many stamens. In the center of the flower is a single pistil with its stigma, style, and ovary.

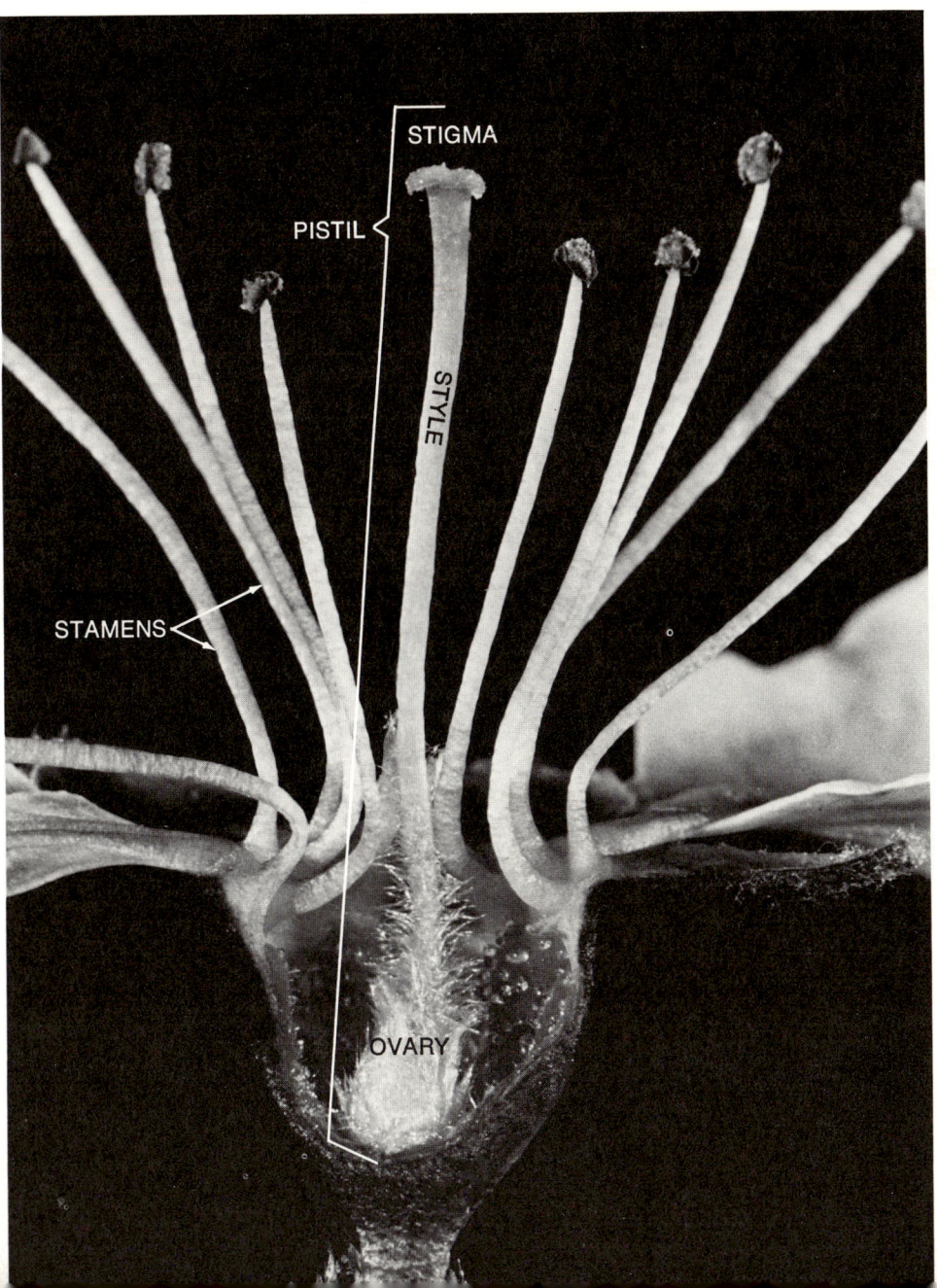

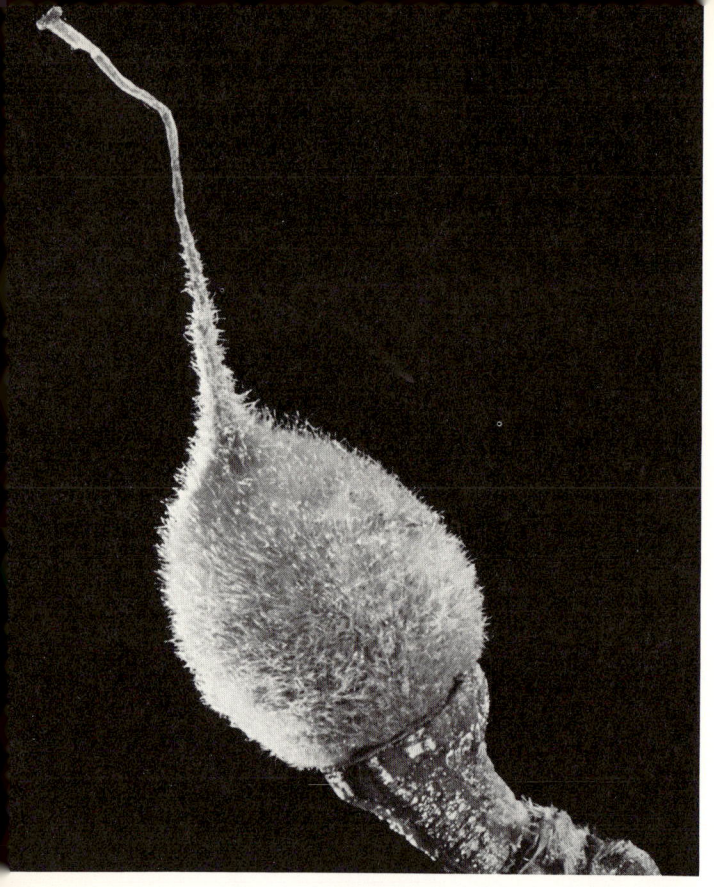

After pollination
and fertilization,
the petals fall,
the flowers fade,
and the ovary develops.
It is hairy
on the outside.

It grows bigger.
In the center,
the seed develops.

Around the seed the inner wall of the ovary becomes woody and turns into a pit of the peach. You can see the pit forming in this picture. Outside the pit the ovary becomes fleshy and juicy.

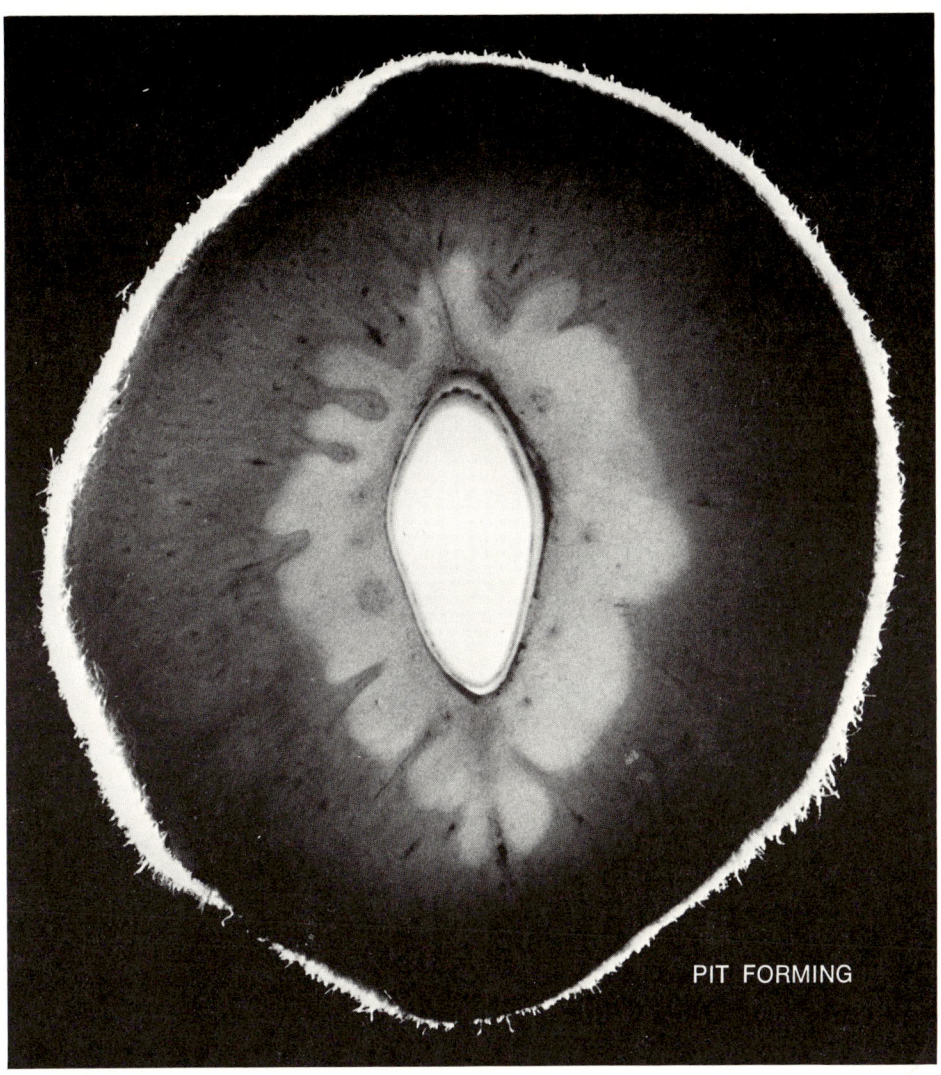

PIT FORMING

Each ovary becomes a ripe peach.

You have to crack open the pit to reach the seed. You can plant it if you treat it first just as you do the apple and pear seeds. But the seed of peach trees also cannot be depended on to produce the same sort of peaches as grew on the parent tree. So peach buds from good varieties usually are grafted onto young trees with strong roots.

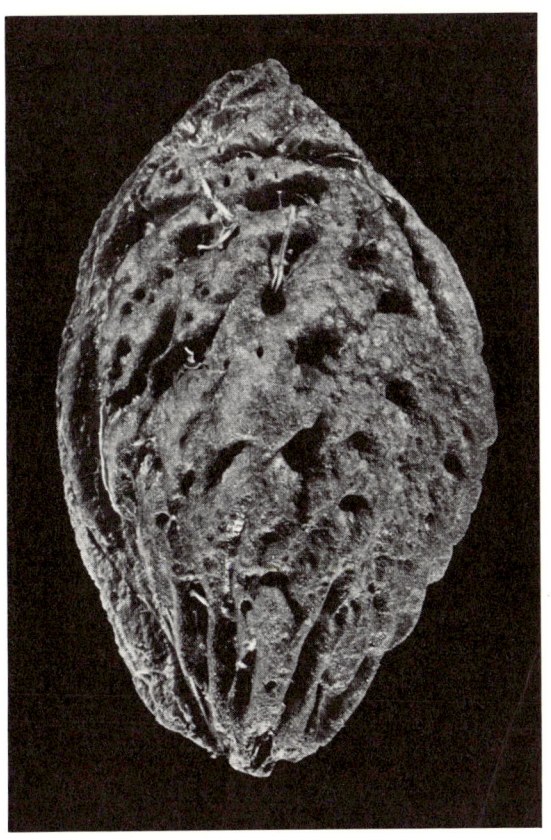 

The ovaries of plum flowers become plum fruits.
Each plum contains a pit that is like the peach pit.
It too comes from the inner wall of the ovary.
The seed is inside the pit.

The ovaries of cherry blossoms become cherry fruits. Each cherry contains a pit that is like peach and plum pits. Again it comes from the inner ovary wall. The seed is inside the pit just as it is in peach and plum fruits.

The ovary of an orange flower becomes an orange. On orange trees you often can see the flowers and fruit together, because the flowers take six to ten months to become fruit. During this long time new blossoms keep opening.

All fruits come from the ovaries of the flowers, and they usually contain seeds. Occasionally there are fleshy parts around the ovary that become part of the fruit as in the case of the apple and pear.

Fruit trees are useful because they produce the fruit we eat, but they are also beautiful to look at when they flower in the spring.